1 MONTH OF
FREE
READING

at
www.ForgottenBooks.com

By purchasing this book you are eligible for one month membership to ForgottenBooks.com, giving you unlimited access to our entire collection of over 700,000 titles via our web site and mobile apps.

To claim your free month visit:
www.forgottenbooks.com/free307533

ISBN 978-0-483-00515-0
PIBN 10307533

OVERSIGHT OF HOME LOAN GUARANTY PROGRAM

Y 4. V 64/3: 103-23

Oversight of Home Loan Guaranty Pro...

HEARING

BEFORE THE

SUBCOMMITTEE ON
HOUSING AND MEMORIAL AFFAIRS

OF THE

COMMITTEE ON VETERANS' AFFAIRS
HOUSE OF REPRESENTATIVES

ONE HUNDRED THIRD CONGRESS

FIRST SESSION

JULY 22, 1993

Printed for the use of the Committee on Veterans' Affairs

Serial No. 103-23

U.S. GOVERNMENT PRINTING OFFICE

74-313 O   WASHINGTON : 1994

For sale by the U S. Government Printing Office
Superintendent of Documents, Congressional Sales Office, Washington, DC 20402
ISBN 0-16-043479-3

OVERSIGHT OF HOME LOAN GUARANTY PROGRAM

HEARING

BEFORE THE

SUBCOMMITTEE ON
HOUSING AND MEMORIAL AFFAIRS

OF THE

COMMITTEE ON VETERANS' AFFAIRS
HOUSE OF REPRESENTATIVES

ONE HUNDRED THIRD CONGRESS

FIRST SESSION

JULY 22, 1993

Printed for the use of the Committee on Veterans' Affairs

Serial No. 103–23

U.S. GOVERNMENT PRINTING OFFICE
74–313 O   WASHINGTON : 1994

For sale by the U S. Government Printing Office
Superintendent of Documents, Congressional Sales Office, Washington, DC 20402
ISBN 0-16-043479-3

COMMITTEE ON VETERANS' AFFAIRS

G.V. (SONNY) MONTGOMERY, Mississippi, *Chairman*

DON EDWARDS, California
DOUGLAS APPLEGATE, Ohio
LANE EVANS, Illinois
TIMOTHY J. PENNY, Minnesota
J. ROY ROWLAND, Georgia
JIM SLATTERY, Kansas
JOSEPH P. KENNEDY, II, Massachusetts
GEORGE E. SANGMEISTER, Illinois
JILL L. LONG, Indiana
CHET EDWARDS, Texas
MAXINE WATERS, California
BOB CLEMENT, Tennessee
BOB FILNER, California
FRANK TEJEDA, Texas
LUIS V. GUTIERREZ, Illinois
SCOTTY BAESLER, Kentucky
SANFORD BISHOP, Georgia
JAMES E. CLYBURN, South Carolina
MIKE KREIDLER, Washington
CORRINE BROWN, Florida

BOB STUMP, Arizona
CHRISTOPHER H. SMITH, New Jersey
DAN BURTON, Indiana
MICHAEL BILIRAKIS, Florida
THOMAS J. RIDGE, Pennsylvania
FLOYD SPENCE, South Carolina
TIM HUTCHINSON, Arkansas
TERRY EVERETT, Alabama
STEVE BUYER, Indiana
JACK QUINN, New York
SPENCER BACHUS, Alabama
JOHN LINDER, Georgia
CLIFF STEARNS, Florida
PETER T. KING, New York

MACK FLEMING, *Staff Director and Chief Counsel*

SUBCOMMITTEE ON HOUSING AND MEMORIAL AFFAIRS

GEORGE E. SANGMEISTER, Illinois, *Chairman*

SANFORD BISHOP, Georgia
MIKE KREIDLER, Washington
G.V. (SONNY) MONTGOMERY, Mississippi

DAN BURTON, Indiana
FLOYD SPENCE, South Carolina
STEVE BUYER, Indiana

(II)

CONTENTS

July 22, 1993

(III)

OVERSIGHT OF HOME LOAN GUARANTY PROGRAM

THURSDAY, JULY 22, 1993

House of Representatives,
Subcommittee on Housing and
Memorial Affairs,
Committee on Veterans' Affairs,
Washington, DC.

The subcommittee met, pursuant to other business, at 9:42 a.m., in room 334, Cannon House Office Building, Hon. George E. Sangmeister (chairman of the subcommittee) presiding.

Present: Representatives Sangmeister, Bishop, Kreidler, Burton, and Buyer.

OPENING STATEMENT OF CHAIRMAN SANGMEISTER

Mr. SANGMEISTER. We will proceed with the hearing this morning.

This morning's hearing is going to focus on the Department of Veterans Affairs Home Loan Guaranty Program. We will discuss the overall state of the program and focus on the implementation of Public Law 102–547.

Those of you that are knowledgeable in this area know that this law expanded VA loan guaranty entitlement to certain members of the Reserves and National Guard, established an adjustable rate mortgage program, permitted the Secretary to allow the veteran and the lender to negotiate the interest rate on VA loans, and enabled the VA to make direct loans to Native American veterans living on trust lands.

Although the law is still relatively new, preliminary information indicates that it is a success. Over the last several years, other enacted laws have also had a significant impact on the home loan program, achieving a sounder financial base, diminishing the need for appropriations, and finetuning the home loan benefit with improvements to service more veterans.

Hopefully, we will discuss the sale of loan assets by the VA, including the way such assets are marketed, the most recent results of loan sales, and plans for future sales. I am also interested in hearing about the VA's efforts in the servicing and property management functions. Servicing and property management are vital parts of the loan guaranty program needing our careful oversight and attention.

I am satisfied by the progress that has been made in the loan guaranty area in the past few years and hope that with the added servicing tool contained in H.R. 949, that the VA can even do a bet-

(1)

ter job next year. H.R. 949 is scheduled for full committee markup next week.

Before we proceed to the witnesses that we have here today, does the gentleman from Indiana have any comments?

Mr. BUYER. I have no statement, Mr. Chairman.

Mr. SANGMEISTER. The gentleman from Washington.

Mr. KREIDLER. No, thank you.

Mr. SANGMEISTER. Nothing. Fine.

Mr. SANGMEISTER. We have two panels today. The first is from the Department of Veterans Affairs. It is always a pleasure to have Mr. Vogel, who is the Deputy Under Secretary for Benefits, here with us, and also Keith Pedigo, who is the Director of the Loan Guaranty Service.

Gentlemen, if you would come forward. We have your written testimony that you have submitted to the committee, which will be made a part of the record. You may proceed.

Mr. Vogel.

STATEMENT OF R.J. VOGEL, DEPUTY UNDER SECRETARY FOR BENEFITS, DEPARTMENT OF VETERANS AFFAIRS, R. KEITH PEDIGO, DIRECTOR, LOAN GUARANTY SERVICE

Mr. VOGEL. Thank you, Mr. Chairman. Good morning.

Mr. SANGMEISTER. Good morning.

Mr. VOGEL. I would like to make a brief summary statement, if I may.

Mr. SANGMEISTER. Go right ahead.

Mr. VOGEL. Mr. Pedigo and I are pleased to appear before you today to discuss the operation of the Loan Guaranty Program.

In your invitation letter, you advised that the primary purpose of the hearing would be to review VA's implementation of Public Law 102–547 which made a number of changes in the Loan Guaranty Program. For the first time, VA home loans were extended to persons whose only service was in the Selected Reserve and the National Guard.

The new law provides for a three-year nationwide test program for ARM's. It also authorizes the Secretary for a three-year period to elect to require that VA guaranteed loans bear an interest rate that is negotiated and agreed upon by the veteran and the lender and authorize veterans to pay reasonable discount points in connection with these loans. New provisions were added to the law for energy-efficient mortgages. VA loans can be increased up to $6,000 above the reasonable value of the property for adding energy-efficient improvements.

The enactment of the law has generated a great deal of interest. For the 6-month period ending April 30, 1993, field stations reported 115,935 loans closed. Of those, 2,400 are adjustable rate mortgages and 114 are energy-efficient mortgages. Certificates of eligibility for the Selected Reserves who became eligible under the new law total in excess of 8,000, and 855 loans were made to these individuals. We fully expect that the volume of those loans will increase, especially as the Reservists and the real estate lending communities become more aware and those 8,000 certificates of eligibility are presented for full participation in the program.

We are carefully monitoring veterans' experience under the new negotiated rate system. The majority of VA-guaranteed acquisition loans were closed at terms which approximate what would have been reasonable had VA still been setting the interest rate.

The law also established a pilot program for direct loans to qualified Native American veterans who wish to purchase, construct, or improve homes on trust lands. We expect to publish interim final regulations to implement this program in the near future. A pamphlet which explains it has been printed and distributed to approximately 650 tribal leaders along with a copy of a prototype memorandum of understanding. We have made contact with tribal leaders in several areas and have a number of MOU's in the negotiation stage.

I would also like to bring you and the committee, Mr. Chairman, up to date on the current activity in the Loan Guaranty Program. With mortgage interest rates as low as they have been in 20 years and the major changes in the program under Public Law 102–547, the number of VA-guaranteed loans made this year has increased significantly. For fiscal year 1993 to date, through May, we have guaranteed 228,845 loans as compared to 171,744 for the same period last year. At that rate, we will guarantee over 300,000 loans this fiscal year.

In the construction and valuation area, even with the unprecedented loan volume, we have been able to process certificates of reasonable value on a very timely basis. Through June, 90 percent of the certificates were issued within 20 days of the request, which is the established minimum timeliness standard.

I am also pleased to report that the trend in defaults and foreclosures is downward. Defaults reported during the first half of fiscal year 1993 were down 9 percent from those reported for the same period in fiscal year 1992 and down 12 percent from those in the same period of fiscal year 1991.

Foreclosures for the first half of fiscal year 1993 were down 20 percent from those reported in the same period in 1992, and 19 percent down from the 1991 numbers. Defaults pending decreased from 122,775 at the end of fiscal year 1991 to 113,654 by the end of fiscal year 1992. The number of defaults reported in those years declined from 167,000 to 153,000.

VBA has encouraged field stations to improve their supplemental servicing by developing a foreclosure avoidance index. That index measures the extent to which foreclosures would have been greater had an alternative to foreclosure not have occurred.

For the first half of this fiscal year, the index shows that approximately 25 percent more foreclosures would have occurred had our regional offices not intervened with loan holders on behalf of veterans or pursued alternatives to foreclosure with veterans.

In assisting veterans with alternatives and reducing program costs, our servicing efforts have showed a savings of over $69 million in fiscal year 1992 and approximately $34 million for the first half of the present fiscal year.

Mr. Chairman, our inventory of properties on hand reached an all-time high of 25,000 in March 1988. Since then, we have seen a steady reduction in the inventory. Property sales for the first 9 months of fiscal year 1993 have generated over $1.3 billion in revenues for the revolving funds, and we have approximately 500 fewer properties on hand now than we did a year ago. In fact, the inventory of 12,300 properties on hand is the lowest it has been in a decade.

Our present sales goals call for a continued inventory reduction as well as an effort to sell the older inventory. This focus on selling older properties has been very successful. By the end of June of 1993, only 807 properties, or 7 percent of the total inventory, were over 12 months old. Five years ago, that number was 3,800.

Mr. Chairman, VA launched its Vinnie Mac securities program in June of 1992 following the enactment of Public Law 102–291. That law authorized VA to directly guarantee the timely payment of principal and interest on mortgage securities issued incident to a sale of VA vendee loans. The new guaranteed certificate sales program was nicknamed Vinnie Mac to establish market recognition for the securities. In 1993, two sales have been completed to date, a February 25 sale for $608 million of vendee loans and a June 24 sale of $576 million in vendee loans. Post-sale analysis indicates——

Mr. BUYER. Mr. Chairman, I missed the first number.

I didn't hear if Mr. Vogel said "million" or "billion."

Mr. VOGEL. Six hundred and eight million dollars in the February sale, sir.

Mr. BUYER. All right. Thank you.

Mr. VOGEL. And $576 million in the June 24 sale.

Our analysis indicates that VA continues to receive significantly better pricing for guaranteed Vinnie Mac mortgage securities issued than that received through previous sales. VA's next Vinnie Mac sale is scheduled for September 1993.

My last area of discussion concerns Loan Guaranty staffing. At the end of May, the Loan Guaranty Program had a total of 2,085 FTEE. That is 18 higher than the 2,067 FTEE estimated for 1993 in the President's fiscal year 1994 budget. For fiscal year 1994, the budget represents 2,042 FTEE, which is a 2 percent decrease over the present employment levels. With those resources, we expect to provide quality and timely service to veterans in fiscal year 1994.

Mr. Chairman, that concludes my statement. I would be pleased to answer any questions which you or other members of the subcommittee might have.

[The prepared statement of Mr. Vogel appears at p. 20.]

Mr. SANGMEISTER. Yes, we have a few.

Apparently from your oral testimony and reading your written testimony, the program has been successful. But has information to the veterans been generated by the VA's own publicity, or has it been through other media accounts? How has the information been disseminated to generate the kind of activity that we are seeing? Has the VA been promoting this?

Mr. VOGEL. The VA's general outreach has been helpful. The lending industry has also helped to get the information out.

With respect to Reservists, information provided by the respective military departments has been very helpful.

I don't know if Mr. Pedigo would like to add to that.

Mr. PEDIGO. Yes, I would. Just a few items.

We initially issued a press release when the bill was signed back in late October of 1992 that detailed the provisions in the bill.

In addition, our field offices issued a release to all participants in our program, the lending institutions and the real estate brokers, laying out the provisions in much greater detail than we had in our press release.

Also, our field offices are required, on an ongoing basis, to conduct seminars with lending institution employees and real estate brokers. That opportunity lets us tell them about the new provisions of this bill.

We think it is a combination of these different types of outreach that have resulted in the large number of loans that have been made under this program.

Mr. SANGMEISTER. So the word got out pretty good then.

Mr. PEDIGO. Yes.

Mr. SANGMEISTER. You stated that for fiscal year 1993 to date, through May, that you have guaranteed 228,000-plus loans as compared to 171,000-plus loans for that same period a year ago. How much of this activity do you attribute to refinancing, and what percentage do you think is attributed to the interest rate reduction loans?

Mr. PEDIGO. Out of that 228,000, I believe there were about 85,000 refinancing loans. The refi's would fall out into two categories. One is the interest rate reduction refinancing loans, and there were about 72,000 of those. Secondly, approximately 13,000 were what we call cash-out refinancing loans.

So basically about 31 or 32 percent of the 228,000 loans were interest rate reduction refinancing loans.

Mr. SANGMEISTER. Okay.

One of the provisions in the law that we are reviewing this morning would create a direct loan program for Native American veterans who reside on trust lands. Why has it taken you so long to draft the regulations to implement this program?

Mr. PEDIGO. When the bill was signed back in October of last year, we began drafting the regulations. They were drafted in the initial form back in January and have been going through the concurrence process since that time.

But the fact that the regs have not been finalized has really not slowed the implementation of the program because our general counsel has told us that we may begin making direct loans under this program as soon as we execute a memorandum of understanding with a Native American organization. We have several of these memoranda that are very close to being executed, and we expect that within the next four to 6 weeks we will be in a position to start making direct loans.

Mr. SANGMEISTER. What is the next step after the rules are put together?

Mr. PEDIGO. What we will probably do is actually make some loans before the regulations are finalized.

Mr. SANGMEISTER. The word is getting out to Native Americans that the program is there. Is that correct?

Mr. PEDIGO. That is correct.

We have conducted a lot of outreach with Native American organizations. We recently sent out a prototype of the memorandum of understanding to about 650 Indian tribes as well as the Hawaiian Homelands and the Alaska Native organizations. In addition, we included a pamphlet that we have drafted that is primarily intended for the Native American population, telling them how to go about utilizing this benefit.

We think that we are doing a good job of getting the word out, and our offices tell us that they have had a lot of inquiries from Native American organizations wanting to begin the negotiation process to get a memorandum of understanding in place, which is the primary prerequisite to making a direct loan under this program.

Mr. SANGMEISTER. Okay. You stated that there were approximately 12,332 properties on hand. That is 500 fewer properties than you had a year ago, your lowest inventory apparently in a decade. This is obviously very commendable. I also note that you are focusing on selling some 807 properties which have been on hand for over 12 months, and out of these properties you indicate you have sold 19 properties to groups sheltering homeless veterans and their families and that you are implementing a test program to lease properties to the homeless.

Could you give us an idea of the location of these properties and to whom they will be leased?

Mr. VOGEL. Mr. Chairman, I can submit for the record the location by city and the number of properties sold under the homeless program, and I can do the same for those to be leased. They are literally coast to coast.

[The information follows:]

The locations designated for VA's lease test program were selected by VA field offices based on their experience with local populations of homeless veterans, local homeless providers, the availability and suitability of properties in the VA inventory, and VA staffing resources to monitor the activities of the providers, as well as the properties under lease. The locations are listed below:

State	Cities	# Properties
NY	New York	1
NJ	Willingboro	1
PA	Pittsburgh	1
VA	Virginia Beach	1
NH	Manchester	1
MD	Baltimore	3
OH	Cleveland, Columbus, Cincinnati & Toledo	5
IN	Indianapolis	2
MI	Detroit	3
MN	Minneapolis & St. Paul	2
KS	Wichita	1
FL	Jacksonville, Miami, Orlando, Pensacola & Tampa	5
NC	Charlotte, Winston-Salem & Raleigh	3
MS	Jackson	1
AR	Little Rock	1
TX	Houston	3
CO	Denver	2
NM	Albuquerque	1
UT	Salt Lake City	2
CA	Oakland, Richmond, Vallejo & Los Angeles	5
AZ	Phoenix & Tucson	5
WA	Seattle	1

To date, 17 properties have been purchased by homeless providers under the homeless program, another 2 properties cited are being used by a VA medical center for a compensated work therapy program. These properties were sold/transferred in the following locations:

State	Cities	# Properties
PA	Corapollis, Pittsburgh & Harrisburg	3
MD	Germantown & Hyattsville	2
WA	Seattle & Tacoma	3
CO	Denver & Westminster	5
OH	Cleveland & Greenville	2
RI	Newport	1
MI	Detroit	2
NH	Manchester	1

Mr. SANGMEISTER. So they are widely spread then, is that right? Is there any certain area that you are concentrating on?

Mr. VOGEL. It is very much across the country based on where the inventory is. There are some areas where we have very little available inventory. It really is very widespread by area and by State.

Mr. SANGMEISTER. If you are going to lease to the homeless, what organizations are you working with?

Mr. VOGEL. Community organizations as well as veterans service organizations who are involved in those efforts as well.

Mr. SANGMEISTER. Working with both.

Mr. VOGEL. Some of the properties that we have sold have been sold to the American Legion and the Jewish War Veterans, but usually it is the homeless groups or homeless coalitions we work with at the community level.

Mr. SANGMEISTER. You stated that 60 percent of your FTEE are involved with servicing delinquent guaranteed and portfolio loans, payment of lenders' claims due to foreclosure and management and disposition of acquired property. Can you tell me how many employees you have involved in servicing delinquent loans?

Mr. PEDIGO. Yes. There are approximately 325 employees who are actually doing loan servicing. We have about 700 employees in the servicing sections around the country, but about half of those are support employees. I would say 300 to 325 are actually doing servicing.

Mr. SANGMEISTER. Is that pretty constant compared to the prior years with all the budget problems? This is an important area. I know you can always use more people, but in your opinion is this adequate to handle the workload?

Mr. PEDIGO. Yes. Actually, that number has increased in recent years with our increased emphasis on servicing loans.

If we have 325 FTEE, which I believe we probably do, then that is probably the highest that we have ever had in the history of the program doing loan servicing. As you said, we would always like to have more and think we can do a better job with more, but we think we are doing a pretty good job with the complement that we have.

Mr. SANGMEISTER. Okay. I see we have a vote coming up, so I would like to finish before we go.

It has been pointed out in your testimony that you refunded 1.8 percent of all foreclosed loans. How do you account for this low percentage, and how many of your refunded loans ultimately go to foreclosure? And, for the record, you did say that almost 75 percent of all the defaults cure either by themselves or intervention. And, to make it a multi-faceted question, how many defaults are reported versus loans actually going to foreclosure?

Do you want to address that?

Mr. PEDIGO. Yes, I would like to.

If we look at fiscal year 1992, we had about 153,000 defaults that were reported. Out of those, about 34,000 actually went to foreclosure and the remainder were reinstated.

The reason the percent of refundings is low is because the program is designed to provide assistance to those veterans who have a lending institution that is no longer willing to forebear but that veteran still has a strong desire to retain the home. The veteran must have been cooperative with both the lender and the VA during the servicing of that delinquent loan, and we limit refundings to those veterans who either presently have the capacity to resume making some level of payment or at some point in the near future will, in all likelihood, have that capacity.

While limiting the refunding to that category of veterans, we still have a termination rate on refunded loans that is presently at 26 percent. If you look at the additional loans that we have refunded in the past that are either seriously delinquent or are in some stage of foreclosure at this time, it is reasonable to conclude that in the near future that termination rate will escalate to somewhere around 35 to 38 percent.

Mr. SANGMEISTER. Okay.

Is it correct to say that almost 75 percent of the defaults either cure themselves——

Mr. PEDIGO. Yes, either cure themselves or are cured with assistance from the VA or the lending institution.

Mr. SANGMEISTER. Okay. How many defaults are reported versus loans actually going to foreclosure? Do you have any figure on that?

Mr. PEDIGO. Last year, we had 153,000 defaults reported and just under 34,000 loans that went to foreclosure.

Mr. SANGMEISTER. I'm sorry, the last figure?

Mr. PEDIGO. Just under 34,000 went to foreclosure.

Mr. SANGMEISTER. The gentleman from Georgia, Mr. Bishop, do you have any questions of this panel?

Mr. BISHOP. Thank you very much, Mr. Chairman, but I don't have any questions at this time.

Mr. SANGMEISTER. Is there anything staff would like to ask?

Mr. JONES. Mr. Chairman, we have no questions. We are concerned, as you are, Mr. Chairman, with the quality of the benefits provided. Undergirding all, of course, is the soundness of the program and the provision of an adequate level of personal to manage it. We will be reviewing the testimony, as you will, sir.

Mr. SANGMEISTER. That is all we have for now. Thank you again for coming over and giving us the information on how the program is going.

We will now recess, go over and vote, and then come back. Meanwhile, if the next panel, the veterans' organizations, would get organized at the table, we can start as soon as we get back.

We will recess for probably 10 to 15 minutes.

(Recess.)

Mr. SANGMEISTER. The subcommittee will reconvene.

We have been over on the Floor where many things happening today, so we appreciate your patience. Everyone is organized here, and we are ready to go. Why don't we just go down the line from right to left.

Let's start with Mr. Dupree of the Paralyzed Veterans of America.

Mr. Dupree, it is always good to see you.

Mr. DUPREE. Good morning, sir.

Mr. SANGMEISTER. Would you proceed, please.

STATEMENTS OF CLIFTON E. DUPREE, ASSOCIATE LEGISLATIVE DIRECTOR, PARALYZED VETERANS OF AMERICA; DENNIS M. CULLINAN, DEPUTY DIRECTOR, NATIONAL LEGISLATIVE SERVICE, VETERANS OF FOREIGN WARS OF THE UNITED STATES; RICHARD F. SCHULTZ, ASSISTANT NATIONAL LEGISLATIVE DIRECTOR, DISABLED AMERICAN VETERANS; MICHAEL P. CLINE, EXECUTIVE DIRECTOR, ENLISTED ASSOCIATION OF THE NATIONAL GUARD OF THE UNITED STATES; AND PAUL S. EGAN, EXECUTIVE DIRECTOR, VIETNAM VETERANS OF AMERICA, INC.

STATEMENT OF CLIFTON E. DUPREE

Mr. DUPREE. Good morning, Mr. Chairman and members of the subcommittee.

Paralyzed Veterans of America thanks you for inviting us to testify today. I want to begin by conveying our gratitude for the time and effort you and the members of your committee have devoted to this program.

The existence of a viable benefit program to assist veterans in purchasing homes remains extremely important to the members of our organization. Limited to accessible housing, individuals using wheelchairs are especially vulnerable to shifts in the national housing market. However, the Department of Veterans Affairs' Home Loan Guaranty Program has, without question, enabled many paralyzed veterans to fulfill their dreams of home ownership.

Since the enactment of the Veterans' Home Loan Amendments of 1992, Public Law 102–547, the VA has guaranteed more than 2,000 adjustable rate mortgages used by veterans to either purchase or refinance their present homes, and the expansion of the VA home loan guaranty entitlement to certain members of the Reserve and National Guard has generated 900 new home loans, and the VA has issued over 8,000 certificates of eligibility.

The Tribal Land Home Loan Program will provide VA direct loans to eligible Native American veterans to purchase, construct, or improve a home on Native American trust lands, and the VA direct loans are limited to the cost of the home or $80,000 whichever is less. However, no home loans have been made to Native American veterans living on trust lands, but a memorandum of understanding from the Secretary of Veterans Affairs on the Tribal Land Home Loan Program has been sent to all tribal nations for their review and approval.

With the pending implementation of these programs, it is more important than ever that resources be made available as was recommended in the independent budget for VA to have an additional 50 VA loan servicing activities—50 FTEE's. During fiscal year 1992, VA's successful direct interventions of 5,029 properties resulted in an estimated $69 million in program savings, and during the first two quarters of 1993 successful interventions on 2,500 properties has already resulted in an estimated program savings of $32 million. This equates.to an annualized savings of $48 million in direct program savings.

Perhaps equally important are the indirect savings to the Government. When the VA regional office actively assists veterans through personal supplemental servicing, they improve service to veteran borrowers in need of advice and assistance. The VA estimates that at least 500 foreclosures are avoided annually through personal servicing assistance which made direct intervention with the lender unnecessary.

Mr. Chairman, this concludes my testimony. I will be pleased to answer any questions you may have.

[The prepared statement of Mr. Dupree appears at p. 31.]

Mr. SANGMEISTER. All right. We will proceed with Mr. Schultz, who is the assistant national legislative director for the Disabled American Veterans.

Welcome.

STATEMENT OF RICHARD F. SCHULTZ

Mr. SCHULTZ. Thank you, Mr. Chairman.

On behalf of the 1.3 million members of the Disabled American Veterans and our Women's Auxiliary, I thank you for the opportunity to appear here today.

At the outset, Mr. Chairman, we must commend you and the members of the subcommittee for the timely exercise of your oversight responsibilities. In addition, we acknowledge and applaud the members of the subcommittee for your outstanding advocacy on behalf of America's veterans. Clearly, had it not been for the advocacy of this subcommittee, loan guaranty benefits available to America's veteran population would have been significantly eroded.

Mr. Chairman, I will now address those provisions of Public Law 102–547 identified in your letter of invitation. We have been advised that during the period of November 1992 through April 1993 there were 855 loans guaranteed by VA for members of the National Guard and Reserves. In addition, about 8,300 certificates of eligibility have been issued by VA, and we also understand that the use of the VA loan guaranty entitlement for the Guard and Reserve is increasing as more become aware of this program. Our only concern, Mr. Chairman, is that VA Loan Guaranty have enough employees to handle any increased workload that may come about as a result of this new entitlement.

With respect to the pilot program for adjustable rate mortgages and the veteran lender negotiated interest rates, quite frankly, we have received no complaints from our members and have no comments other than that we will continue to monitor these two pilot programs.

Mr. Chairman, we understand that VA also intends to issue interim regulations regarding the Native American Direct Loan Program, and they expect to be able to make some loans in the near future. We believe that the Native American Home Loan Pilot Program has the potential to provide a meaningful benefit to an underserved population of America's veterans, and we applaud the subcommittee for its efforts in this regard.

In the area of loan servicing, we understand the VA has made great strides over the past several years. Effective loan servicing just makes good sense. In human terms, proper loan servicing can prevent a veteran and his or her family from becoming another homeless statistics. In economic terms, effective loan servicing saves taxpayers' money.

During fiscal year 1992, VA successfully intervened in 5,029 loan defaults, saving more than $69 million in taxpayer dollars. The statistics for the first half of fiscal year 1993 show that a repeat of last year will probably happen.

In an effort to reduce the housing inventory, VA has engaged in a number of activities which include paid advertising, outreach to realtors, seminars for the real estate community, and, in addition, they have made use of some computer technology, such as the bulletin board in certain high-volume areas of the country, in an effort to appraise would-be buyers of the availability of VA properties.

We commend the VA for its efforts in the property management area and would hope that they continue to expand their efforts. We also understand that there has been a slight increase in processing time due in part to increased loan activity.

We would like to comment that the loan appraisal process, the LAP program, which began in fiscal year 1992 is starting to reap some dividends, and for the period of April 1, 1992, through March 31, 1993, there were 7,374 determinations of reasonable value processed using the LAP program.

With respect to efforts regarding loan asset sales, we note that in February 1992 VA realized increased income for loan asset sales of about $12.5 million, and thus far in fiscal year 1993 VA has realized nearly a $20 million increase in revenue as a result of the enactment of Public Law 102–291.

Mr. Chairman, dealing with the issue of FTEE, the DAV, as well as the independent budget VSO's, have recommended an increase of 50 employees in the loan servicing area, and, as I previously mentioned, effective loan servicing reaps many dividends both in human and economic terms.

Thank you, Mr. Chairman. I would be happy to answer any questions you may have.

[The prepared statement of Mr. Schultz appears at p. 37.]

Mr. SANGMEISTER. Okay.

Mr. Cullinan from the Veterans of Foreign Wars.

STATEMENT OF DENNIS M. CULLINAN

Mr. CULLINAN. Thank you, Mr. Chairman.

On behalf of the 2.8 million members of the Veterans of Foreign Wars and its Ladies' Auxiliary, we wish to thank you for inviting us to take part in today's hearing with respect to the VA Home Loan Program and the implementation of Public Law 102–547.

As you know, the VFW has been a staunch supporter of this highly successful veterans' program through the years, and we are both pleased and gratified to play a role in today's discussion.

As you are, of course, aware, Public Law 102–547 represents a significant enhancement of the VA Home Loan Program. It is a matter of record that, with the exception of opening up the VA Home Loan Program to members of the Reserve and National Guard who have not performed sufficient active duty to be deemed veterans under title 38, the VFW highly supported this law to improve and enhance the service the VA Home Loan Program provides to America's veterans.

Since this Public Law has only been recently enacted, we have accumulated little information from our membership regarding its effect on them. Even so, it is clear that this Public Law is highly beneficial and will certainly enhance the operation of the program and the service it provides veterans.

We would strongly recommend, however, that this Public Law be amended to allow for points to be rolled into a loan when a veteran refinances his home. It is clear from the language contained in the committee report that it was not the intention of the Congress to preclude points from being rolled into refinanced loans, and we offer our strong support for remedial legislation.

Today the subcommittee is also focusing on loan servicing, property management, staffing levels, timeliness, and loan asset sales. In this regard, I cannot overemphasize the VFW's conviction that personal contact between a veteran borrower who has come upon financial hard times and VA is the most effective means of curing defaults. Successful intervention produces compassionate and cost-effective alternatives to foreclosure, such as loan reinstatements, refunding, or voluntary conveyances, also known as deeds in lieu of foreclosure, for problem claims.

Additionally, VA can also sometimes arrange for a loan holder to grant a period of grace to a veteran who has suffered a temporary setback and who will soon be able to resume making loan payments. As is indicated in the veterans' service organizations' independent budget for VA, "Rarely do goals of deficit reduction, program integrity, and efficiency, and good service to veterans coincide so exactly as they do on improving loan servicing."

The VFW couldn't agree more with this point of view, and we too recommend that an additional 50 employees be added to the Loan Servicing Department of VA. It just makes sense. It is better for veterans, better for the VA Home Loan Program.

Mr. Chairman, that concludes my statement.

[The prepared statement of Mr. Cullinan appears at p. 33.]

Mr. SANGMEISTER. Thank you.

Paul Egan from the Vietnam Veterans of America—Paul, welcome.

STATEMENT OF PAUL S. EGAN

Mr. EGAN. Thank you, Mr. Chairman.

First of all, on Public Law 102–547, as we all know, interest rates for quite some time now have been low and are currently in decline, and we believe that it is still a bit premature to pass judgment on the success of this law.

I think it is safe to say that just about anything that we might have done, that the Congress might have done, in the last 18 to 24 months would look pretty good in this market with these interest rates. So once we have seen a cycle where rates have begun to inch up again and we see the data accumulated on that basis, it would probably be better—we would all be in a better position to draw some conclusion as to the success of the law.

When that data are in, I think it is important to ask, for example, whether or not VA's market share of the overall home buying market has increased: Are veterans borrowing more than they can afford using adjustable rate mortgages? And we won't know that until we see an inching up of interest rates. Are they being qualified for mortgages improperly? Are negotiated rates more or less favorable than they were prior to enactment of the law? Are bankers more receptive to veterans now than they were prior to the law? Those are the questions, it seems to my organization, that are in need of answering over a longer period to determine the success of this statute.

I would like to bring the subcommittee's attention to one other matter. Obviously, we are all looking at fiscally constrained times, and there is something that might do with a bit of improvement from the VA, and it is the way in which the VA manages its property and its loan sales. When the VA acquires a property after a foreclosure, it does that quite frequently, and it is often very expensive; $2.2 billion in appropriations were needed between 1984 and 1989 to cover the cost of acquiring some 208,813 deeds.

As you know, we happen to believe that the VA would do better by acquiring not all but more loans instead of deeds, but, be that as it may, when the VA sells property in its inventory, it can do it in either of four different ways. It can do it by cash sales, and that is a fairly simple transaction, or it can do term sales which involve installment contracts, mortgages, or deeds of trust.

Installment contracts, if they go into default, the problem can be solved relatively quickly. Not so with mortgages or deeds of trust. Those mortgages or deeds of trust require foreclosure, and there is a process that is used. The loan guaranty section at the regional office asks for help from the VA district counsel or from the U.S. attorney or a fee attorney.

Foreclosures in that process are fairly slow, probably for a variety of reasons, many of which are not the fault of the VA itself, but the fact is that some of these defaults are ranging over extraordinarily long periods of time, which is exactly the problem that you raised, Mr. Chairman, in questioning the wisdom of refinancings as opposed to an adjudicative process for applications for refinancing.

I have a quarterly report ending April 30, 1993, and the arrearages, the number of months of arreagages, ranged from, just on the first page here—these are the number of months in delinquency— 159 months, 99 months, 90 months, 62 months, 37 months, 71 months, 52 months, 57 months, and on and on down the line. On just the first page here, we are talking about foregone assets to the VA in excess of over $400,000. This is a rather lengthy report, and I would be more than willing to share it with the subcommittee.

But it would seem to us that the VA could probably help itself and save itself some money, a considerable amount of money, perhaps even billions, if it would exercise the use when it sells its properties of unrecorded quitclaim deeds so that it were to more aggressively use installment contracts. It can resolve problems of properties that are in default more quickly and more efficiently, and if there is significant revenue to be saved in that, foregone revenue, then I would suggest that at least some portion of that revenue be allocated. As some of my other colleagues have said, to the addition of new home loan servicing personnel to do more of what it is already doing and doing a fairly good job of, which is servicing loans in default by veterans who are simply using their guarantees as opposed to individuals who have purchased properties directly from the VA.

That concludes my summary, Mr. Chairman, and I would be pleased to answer your questions.

[The prepared statement of Mr. Egan appears at p. 44.]

Mr. SANGMEISTER. Thank you.

Michael Cline of the Enlisted Association of the National Guard of the United States—welcome.

STATEMENT OF MICHAEL P. CLINE

Mr. CLINE. Thank you, Mr. Chairman. We are pleased to have the opportunity to submit testimony before the Veterans' Affairs Subcommittee on Housing and Memorial Affairs. We probably express the views of more than 450,000 enlisted National Guard members of the United States.

Mr. Chairman, I would like to take this opportunity to thank you and this subcommittee for the successful markup of H.R. 821 this morning. This will go a long way in bringing the Guard and Reserve into the total force picture, and I am sure those 2,500 men and women who are currently battling the mighty Mississippi are going to feel very proud of this news.

Mr. Chairman, we are here today to talk a little bit about Public Law 102–547. My comments will be basically restricted to how it is affecting the National Guard and the Reserve components. Basically, we have found that the word has been slow in getting out to the National Guard and Reserve community.

One of my counterparts from NCOA yesterday met with Ms. Debbie Levy, Assistant Secretary for Defense, Reserve Affairs, and she has assured us that she is going to do everything she can at her Department level to get the word out even further.

Basically, the word that the VA has gotten out has somewhere along the line been stagnated. Out of the roughly 530,000 enlisted members of the National Guard and over 1,200,000 members of the Reserve component altogether, 8,000 eligibilities are really a low amount, but if you take a look at the short period of time, I guess we could probably say that is a significant foothold, especially when 855 loans have been approved in an 8-month period of time.

The other thing, Mr. Chairman, is, earlier this year I had the privilege of using my VA loan guaranty from my prior service years to purchase a home, and during that time I talked to various relatives, and the word had been slow getting out to the real estate market on this program. Most realtors knew that there was a program that Guard and Reserve members after 6 years were eligible for, but they did not understand the fact that the Guard and Reserve member had to pay a premium for the program. We view this program as a way it is going to assure the success of the program for the future.

As far as the adjustable rate mortgage, Mr. Chairman, being a real estate person, having dealt with VA home loans and VA repossessed homes in the past, the adjustable rate mortgage in the real estate market is a good way for young people to buy into real estate. It lets them come in with what their current means are, and assuming that their means in the future are going to be there to adjust their payments. As long as there is a cap that is put on these loans that it is not going to exceed a certain amount, we foresee no future problem as the private industry has seen over the past years.

In regard to the trust for our American Indians, I would like to make note that the president of the Enlisted Association of the National Guard of the United States is a full-blooded Cherokee Indian and owns property out in Oklahoma along with his wife, and I assure you that our Native Americans deserve every bit of what we give them and more.

Mr. Chairman, that concludes my testimony.

[The prepared statement of Mr. Cline appears at p. 40.]

Mr. SANGMEISTER. Thank you.

I hear one theme that seems to come from all of you, and that is whether there are enough people assigned to loan servicing. It is my understanding that the veterans' independent budget is going to recommend 50 new employees. So I would think that if that goes through we will be able to fill the gap.

Is there any other particular issue? As I said, I get the feeling from all of you, except for perhaps Mr. Egan, that there need to be significant improvements here. Is there any individual thing you can contribute that you have heard from your members that could improve this whole situation, or is it a little bit early to make any further analysis of where we are? I didn't really pick up anything from you, outside of a need for more employees, that is crucial.

Mr. CULLINAN. Mr. Chairman, I would add one thing. Before this hearing, I spoke with our chief field representative, trying to get some information from the field about the impact of this law and the operation of the VA Home Loan Program in general. There wasn't too much to say about this specific law. However, there is an indication that loan servicing, the perception and reality of loan servicing in the field, has improved considerably. They paid particular attention to Houston. Houston was a real problem zone a while back. According to our folks, they are saying that VA is doing a much better job. So I think that is something that should be said at this time.

Mr. SANGMEISTER. Okay. We appreciate that.

Mr. Egan, do you have anything further? As I understand your testimony, you are delaying judgment as to whether the program is operating correctly or not.

Mr. EGAN. Mr. Chairman, if we had participated in the deliberations on the adjustable rate mortgages and negotiated interest rates, we would have opposed them simply because past history in a period of high and rising interest rates proved to be devastating to a great number of not only veterans but homeowners with adjustable rate mortgages to begin with.

Mr. SANGMEISTER. Mr. Cline said he thought the adjustable rate mortgages were the way to go. You don't agree with that?

Mr. EGAN. I am saying what we would have expressed at the time that the legislation creating the adjustable rate mortgages would have been opposition, and it is a fact, the law is the law, and we are reserving judgment on it. We hope it works.

Obviously, if someone can get into a home and afford to make the payments even when the rates go up in a period where interest rates are rising, then that is all to the good, because getting into the home in the first place is very important, but getting into a property you ultimately can't afford that ultimately goes into default and may face foreclosure is not something that we think is particularly positive. We are reserving judgment.

Mr. SANGMEISTER. Okay. If there is nothing else that anyone has, I don't have any other particular questions. We have your testimony, written and oral. We will review it. I get the opinion this morning that, basically, the program is proceeding very well and that most of the organizations approve of the way the VA has been working, with the possible exception of the Vietnam Veterans' organizations. Is that a correct analysis?

Mr. CLINE. Mr. Chairman, I would like to make one comment. Currently, there is some legislation pending, H.R. 2331. I have some concerns about that piece of legislation. In talking to the VA, I found out that there is a possibility that this piece of legislation could ultimately cost the VA some significant amount of dollars. It could possibly stall the foreclosure process by letting people stay in their houses during a trial period of time where the VA would do the refunding bit.

One thing that concerns me, though, is, if this bill passes, and based on conversations with the VA, it could enormously affect the amount of staff that the VA is going to have to have if this bill is passed to service these loans.

Mr. SANGMEISTER. I can assure you, Mr. Cline, we are taking a very careful look at that piece of legislation. Some of the concerns you have raised are some of the same that we have, and we are trying to get figures and facts put together as to what the input of that would be.

Next week we are having a general markup of the full committee on H.R. 949, my bill. That is one approach toward helping the situation. I don't know what is going to happen at committee, whether there will be amendments offered to my bill or not, but we will have to face that. I share the same concerns, and I am happy to have you say that.

Mr. Egan.

Mr. EGAN. Thank you, Mr. Chairman.

I think concern with prolonged defaults—excessive numbers of months in which individuals are in properties while the properties are in default—is something that everyone shares. Part of the point of my oral testimony, Mr. Chairman, was to demonstrate that in the case of the very process that the VA is using today in disposing of its property in its inventory of foreclosed properties, that the monthly delinquencies are far more excessive than anything even remotely contemplated in the legislation introduced by Mr. Evans and Mr. Kennedy. Since Mr. Cline raised the issue of the bill, I feel obligated to respond in that way.

Mr. SANGMEISTER. I was sure you would. I don't think we need to, at this hearing, get into a discussion of how that will be ironed out probably next Tuesday.

Just as a thought on the foreclosures that you are talking about, as I understand it from the VA, there are obviously some problems with property that is in foreclosure. For example, almost 24 percent of the veterans don't even own the property; 20 percent of them have abandoned the property; in 13.5 percent the property is worth less than the remaining debt; although somewhat included in the previous numbers, 41 percent of the time the VA is, unable to make personal contact with the borrower. However, there are a lot of problems in foreclosures that really are out of the hands of the VA. If you can't work with the veteran, you are going to have those kinds of problems. Would you care to comment on that? You don't. Okay.

If there is nothing else, again, thank you all. It is very helpful to hear from all of our organizations as to how things are working, make it all part of the record, and get a review put together. Thank you all very much for coming.

If there is nothing further, the subcommittee is adjourned.

[Whereupon, at 10:57 a.m., the subcommittee was adjourned.]

APPENDIX

PREPARED STATEMENT OF CHAIRMAN SANGMEISTER

This morning's hearing will focus on the Department of Veterans Affairs Home Loan Guaranty Program. We will discuss the overall state of the program and focus on the implementation of Public Law 102–547.

This law expanded VA loan guaranty entitlement to certain members of the Reserves and National Guard, established an adjustable rate mortgage program, permitted the Secretary to allow the veteran and the lender to negotiate the interest rate on VA loans, and enabled the VA to make direct loans to Native American veterans living on trust lands.

Although the law is still relatively new, preliminary information indicates that it is a success. Over the last several years, enacted laws have also had a significant impact on the home loan program—achieving a sounder financial base, diminishing the need for appropriations, and finetuning the home loan benefit with improvements to service more veterans.

Hopefully, we will discuss the sale of loan assets by the VA, including the way such assets are marketed, the most recent results of loan sales and plans for future sales. I am also interested in hearing about VA's efforts in the servicing and property management functions. Servicing and property management are vital parts of the loan guaranty program needing our careful oversight and attention.

I am satisfied by the progress that has been made in the loan guaranty area in the past few years and hope that with the added servicing tool contained in H.R. 949, that the VA can even do a better job next year. H.R. 949 is scheduled for full committee markup next week.

Before I welcome the first panel, I would like to recognize the Ranking Minority Member of the Subcommittee, Dan Burton.

STATEMENT OF R.J. VOGEL

DEPUTY UNDER SECRETARY FOR BENEFITS

DEPARTMENT OF VETERANS AFFAIRS

BEFORE THE

SUBCOMMITTEE ON HOUSING AND MEMORIAL AFFAIRS

COMMITTEE ON VETERANS' AFFAIRS

HOUSE OF REPRESENTATIVES

JULY 22, 1993

Mr. Chairman and Members of the Subcommittee:

I am pleased to appear before you today to discuss the operation of the Department of Veterans Affairs Loan Guaranty Program. In your invitation letter, you advised that the primary purpose of the hearing would be to review VA's implementation of Public Law 102-547. Specific testimony was also requested on loan servicing, property management, staffing levels, timeliness, and loan asset sales.

On October 28, 1992, the President signed Public Law 102-547, the Veterans Home Loan Program Amendments of 1992. This law made a number of changes to the Loan Guaranty Program. For the first time, VA home loans were extended to persons whose only service was in the Selected Reserve or National Guard. Individuals who served at least 6 years became eligible. A funding fee of 2 percent is required, and can be reduced to 1.5 percent with a 5 percent downpayment or 1.25 percent with a 10 percent downpayment. The new law also provided for a 3-year nationwide test program on adjustable rate mortgages (ARMs). The VA ARM program provides for a maximum annual interest rate increase of 1 percent and a 5 percent life of the loan limit on rate increases. We are requiring that applications for ARM loans be underwritten at 1 percentage point above the initial interest rate to reduce the potential risk of rising rates.

(20)

VA-guaranteed home loans have historically been made at or below a maximum interest .rate established by the Secretary pursuant to 38 U.S.C. §§ 3703(c) and 3712(f). Public Law 102-547 authorizes the Secretary of Veterans Affairs to elect to require that such loans bear interest at a rate that is negotiated and agreed upon by the veteran and the lender. This authority is for a 3-year period ending December 31, 1995. The law also authorizes veterans to pay reasonable discount points in connection with these loans. However, these points may not be financed. H.R. 949, which is pending in the current session of Congress, would restore the veteran's' ability to finance discount points on interest rate reduction refinancing loans and certain other loans. As we testified before your Subcommittee on March 4, 1993, VA favors this amendment.

New provisions were added to the law for Energy Efficient Mortgages (EEMs). VA loans can be increased above reasonable value for the purpose of adding energy efficient improvements to the home by up to $3,000 based solely on the cost of improvements, or by up to $6,000 if the increase in the monthly payment does not exceed the likely reduction in monthly utility costs. There will be no additional charge to the veteran's guaranty entitlement as a result of the loan amount increase.

Enactment of Public Law 102-547 has generated a great deal of interest in the VA Home Loan Program. For the 6-month period ending April 30, 1993, field stations reported 115,935 loans closed, of those 2,416 are adjustable rate mortgages and 114 are energy efficient mortgages. Certificates of eligibility issued to Selected Reservists who became eligible under the new law totaled 8,262. Eight hundred and fifty-five loans were made to these individuals. When these data were compiled by our field stations, another 30,000 closed loans had not yet been processed. We fully expect that the volume of loans in all categories will rise, especially those to Reservists as more and more of the over 8,000 Reservists who received certificates of eligibility actually purhase homes with VA-guaranteed loans.

We are carefully monitoring veterans' experiences under the new negotiated rate system to determine the interest rate and points being charged veterans as compared to individuals obtaining FHA insured and conventional loans. The majority of VA-guaranteed acquisition loans were closed at terms which approximate what would have been reasonable terms had VA still been setting maximum interest rates. In December, for example, when quotes for Government National Mortgage Association mortgaged-backed securities averaged around 2-3 points for 8 percent loans, 74 percent of the VA loans surveyed were closed at or below 8 percent with no more than 3 points. The effective interest rate of an 8 percent loan with 3 points is 8.32 percent. In comparison, the average FHA effective interest rate reported for December was 8.54 percent, and the average effective interest rate reported for conventional loans in December was 7.81 percent. In addition, 81 percent of the acquisition loans surveyed from November through April were closed with the veteran paying no points. Overall, our survey shows that the actual effective VA interest rates were slightly less than FHA in 1 month, approximately even in 3 months, and slightly higher than FHA in 2 months. A trend toward lower rates is seen for all three types of loans from November 1992 through April 1993, and the decline in VA rates over the period, 0.72 percent, is exactly the same as for FHA loans and greater than the 0.53 percent decline in conventional interest rates.

With the enactment of Public Law 102-547, the Department of Veterans Affairs is now authorized to make direct loans to qualified Native American veterans who wish to purchase or construct homes on trust land. Interim final regulations to. implement this program are now in the concurrence process, and we expect that they will be published in the Federal Register later this summer. We have drafted a prototype of the Memorandum of Understanding (MOU) to be signed by VA, the

Department of the Interior, and appropriate officials of the Native American tribe or other entity whose lands are held in trust by the United States. A pamphlet which explains the program has been printed and distributed to approximately 650 tribal leaders, along with a copy of the prototype MOU. We have made contact with tribal leaders in several areas, and have a number of MOUs in the negotiation stage.

Mr. Chairman, I would now like to bring you up-to-date on the current activity of the loan guaranty program. With mortgage interest rates as low as they have been in 20 years and the major changes to the program made by Public Law 102-547, the number of VA-guaranteed home loans made this year has increased significantly. In fact, the 93,066 loans guaranteed during the second quarter of FY 1993 is the largest number for any quarter since the last quarter of FY 1987. For FY 1993 year-to-date through May, we have guaranteed 228,845 loans, as compared to 171,744 loans for the same period last year. At this rate, VA will guaranty over 300,000 loans this fiscal year.

In the Construction and Valuation area of the Loan Guaranty Program, even with the unprecedented loan volume, we have been able to process Certificates of Reasonable Value on a very timely basis nationwide. For FY 1993 through June, 90 percent of the certificates were issued within 20 days of the request, which is the established timeliness standard.

I would like to update the Subcommittee on our Lender Appraisal Processing Program (LAPP). Our second annual report to Congress on LAPP, which covered the 12-month period from April 1, 1992, through March 31, 1993, shows a significant increase in lender participation. During that period, VA guaranteed 7,374 loans in which the lender made a determination of reasonable value for the property which secures the loan. This compares favorably with the 607 LAPP loans guaranteed during the initial 6-month period ending March 31, 1992. The number of LAPP loans closed during the last report period suggests that lender participation will continue to increase in the upcoming months. We believe LAPP is providing its principal benefit to our veterans, that of speedier loan closings. Public Law 102-547 extended the authority for LAPP to December 31, 1995.

Mr. Chairman, I am pleased to report that the trend in defaults and foreclosures is downward. Defaults reported during the first half of FY 1993 (76,711) were down 9 percent from those reported in the same period in FY 1992 (84,175) and down 12 percent from those reported in the same period in FY 1991 (87,372). Foreclosures for the first half of FY 1993 (13,513) were down 20 percent from those reported in the same period in FY 1992 (16,880), and were down 19 percent from those reported in FY 1991 (16,605). Defaults pending decreased from 122,775 at the end of FY 1991 to 113,654 at the end of FY 1992. The number of defaults reported in those years declined from 166,945 to 153,389.

In addition to the above, VA has always believed that personal supplemental loan servicing assists veterans to retain homeownership and mitigates VA's program losses through a reduced number of loan terminations and claim payments. Program losses can be reduced when veterans cooperate with VA in resolving insoluble defaults through lower-cost alternatives to foreclosure, such as a private sale or voluntary conveyance of their property.

During FY 1989, VBA's Houston Pilot Project measured the impact of supplemental servicing on delinquent VA-guaranteed loans. For purposes of evaluating the Project, an index was developed--Foreclosure Avoidance with VA Involvement Ratio (FAVIR). The index related specific alternatives to foreclosure to the volume of defaults reported. Components of the index were: Successful VA Interventions (direct VA intervention with a loan holder on behalf of a veteran to obtain forbearance and/or a repayment plan, resulting in reinstatement of the loan); Refunding (purchase of delinquent

VA-guaranteed loans for VA's own portfolio); Compromise Claims (private property sales of property worth less than the amount owing on the mortgage, with VA paying the balance due); and, Deeds in lieu of foreclosure (accepting direct conveyance of property in order to avoid foreclosure of the loan).

The measurement indicators clearly showed that the Project was cost-effective and assisted veterans. Based on the success of the Houston Pilot Project, VBA encouraged all field stations to improve their supplemental servicing by publicizing the FAVIR index and establishing Department goals to improve performance measured by that index. The original index has now evolved into the Foreclosure Avoidance Through Servicing (FATS) index. The new index measures the extent to which foreclosures would have been greater had an alternative to foreclosure not occurred.

For the first half of FY 1993, the FATS index shows that approximately 25 percent more foreclosures would have occurred had our regional offices not intervened with loan holders on behalf of veterans or pursued alternatives to foreclosure with veterans.

In assisting veterans with alternatives to foreclosure and reducing program costs, our servicing efforts showed savings of over $69 million in FY 1992 and approximately $34 million for the first half of FY 1993.

Mr. Chairman, VA's inventory of properties on hand reached an all-time high of 25,172 in March 1988. Since then, we have continued to focus on a steady, measured reduction in the inventory. We have acquired approximately 3,600 fewer properties during the first 9 months of Fiscal Year 1993 than we acquired during the same period in Fiscal Year 1992, and sales for the first 9 months of Fiscal Year 1993 have exceeded acquisitions by 6 percent. Property sales for the first 9 months of Fiscal Year 1993 have generated over $1.3 billion in revenues for the revolving funds, and we have approximately

500 fewer properties on hand now than we did 1 year ago. In fact, the inventory of 12,332 properties on hand is the lowest it has been in over a decade.

Our present sales goals call for a continued modest inventory reduction from the end of Fiscal Year 1992; i.e., that the property inventory at the end of Fiscal Year 1993 not exceed the number of properties on hand as of June 30, 1992, as well as an effort to sell the older inventory so that the number of properties carried more than 12 months will not comprise more than 5 percent of the total number of properties on hand. This focus on selling older properties has been very successful. As of the end of June 1993, only 807 properties (or 7 percent of the total inventory) had been on hand for over 12 months. This is a tremendous reduction from the over 12-month inventory of more than 3,800 properties which we had only 5 years ago.

Now, let me turn to our efforts to assist the homeless. The Homeless Veterans Comprehensive Service Programs Act of 1992 (Public Law 102-590) amended section 3735, title 38, United States Code, to provide authority until December 31, 1995, for the program of using VA-acquired properties to shelter homeless veterans and their families. The legislative history of the homeless program indicated that use of acquired properties for the homeless was intended to assist VA in selling "hard-to-sell" properties. Based on informal discussions with homeless providers, we developed alternative criteria for determining property eligibility and price which were consistent with the statute and instituted a time-phased series of progressive discounts (ranging from 5 to 50 percent) based on the length of time that properties have been available for sale. Under the program, local government agencies and nonprofit organizations, including veterans' organizations, working on behalf of homeless persons, can purchase VA-acquired properties at discounts of as much as 50 percent. To date, 19 properties have been sold under the program and another 2 properties are being used by a VA medical center for a compensated work therapy program. Purchasers include the American Legion, the American GI Forum, the Jewish War Veterans, and other veterans' groups.

The recent law provides authority not only to continue to sell, but also to lease, lease with an option to purchase, or donate acquired properties. The law also authorizes VA to establish credit standards for the sale of properties with vendee loans to local government agencies and nonprofit organizations, including veterans' organizations, working on behalf of homeless persons. We recently implemented a test program to lease 50 properties to homeless providers. Locations of the properties to be leased were selected by VA field offices based on their experience with the local populations of homeless veterans, local homeless providers, the availability and suitability of properties in the VA inventory, and VA staffing resources to monitor the activities of the providers as well as to monitor the properties under lease. Instructions to field offices regarding donation of properties and financing of certain sales to homeless providers have been prepared. We expect to be able to release these instructions within the next 30 to 45 days.

Mr. Chairman, VA launched its "Vinnie Mac" securities program in June 1992 following enactment of Public Law 102-291 on May 20, 1992. That law specifically authorized VA to directly guaranty the timely payment of principal and interest on mortgage securities issued incident to the sale of VA vendee loans.

In order to distinguish the new guaranteed certificate sales from VA's prior vendee loan securitizations through American Housing Trusts, a new issuing vehicle named "Vendee Mortgage Trust" was created. The program itself was nicknamed "Vinnie Mac" to establish market recognition for the VA-guaranteed Real Estate Mortgage Investment Conduit (REMIC) securities as an Agency security comparable to those guaranteed by the Government National Mortgage Association (Ginnie Mae), which are backed by the full faith and credit of the United States of America.

Two VA-guaranteed REMIC pass-through issuances were completed in 1992 under the new "Vinnie Mac" program--a June 25, 1992, sale of $390,872,983 of vendee loans through Vendee Mortgage Trust 1992-1 and a sale of $443,523,580 of vendee loans through Vendee Mortgage Trust 1992-2 on August 27, 1992.

Post-sale analyses of the "Vinnie Mac" sales indicated that VA obtained pricing improvements greater than those projected at the time the authorizing legislation was enacted. It had been anticipated that the certificate guaranty would improve pricing by approximately 0.625 percent, or $5 million per $800 million in sales. VA actually obtained increased proceeds of approximately $12.751 million (1.528 percent) on the approximately $834.4 million in 1992 "Vinnie Mac" sales.

Following completion of these sales, VA's authority to guaranty vendee loan securities was extended to December 31, 1995, by provisions of Public Law 102-547. As a result, VA has continued its "Vinnie Mac" security program for 1993 vendee loan sales. Two such sales have been completed to date--a February 25, 1993, sale of $608,186,422 of vendee loans through Vendee Mortgage Trust 1993-1 and a sale of $576,866,731 of vendee loans through Vendee Mortgage Trust 1993-2 which closed on June 24th. Post-sale analyses indicate that VA continues to receive significantly better pricing for guaranteed "Vinnie Mac" mortgage securities than that obtainable for comparable nonguaranteed securities issued through VA's previous American Housing Trust sale program. Increased proceeds to VA on the $1,185,053,153 of 1993 "Vinnie Mac" sales to date are estimated to be $19.429 million (1.6395 percent).

VA's next "Vinnie Mac" sale is scheduled for September 1993.

Mr. Chairman, I would now like to discuss the progress and achievements of the Lender Monitoring Unit. The Monitoring Unit was created in September 1989 to ensure a higher level of compliance by lenders with the laws, regulations, and policies governing the origination and servicing of VA-guaranteed loans. The first originating lender audit was conducted by the Unit in March 1990, and the first servicing lender audit was conducted in November 1991. As of June 30, 1993, the Unit has completed 525 on-site reviews of lenders and servicers. Four hundred and twenty-two (422) of these reviews were origination audits and 103 were servicing audits. During Fiscal Year 1993, a total of 233 audits will be performed.

Loan Guaranty Service has released 198 origination and 44 servicer final audit reports to lenders. As a result of these reports VA has:

* recovered losses in the amount of $731,234;

* accepted indemnification agreements in the amount of $2,139,836; and

* denied liability on loans with potential claim and acquisition costs totaling $644,940.

The Monitoring Unit also coordinates Loan Guaranty's review of cases from lender audits conducted by the VA Office of Inspector General and the recovery of losses resulting from those cases. As a result of finalized OIG audits, $1,290,561 has been collected for noncompliance with VA credit standards. Additionally, VA has been absolved of potential liability on $251,366 in loans.

My last area of discussion is in response to your request for information on Loan Guaranty staffing. At the end of May the Loan Guaranty Program had a total staffing level of 2,085 FTE fiscal year-to-date through May. This is 18 FTE higher than the 2,067 FTE estimated for FY 1993 in the President's FY 1994 Budget. Approximately 40 percent of these employees are involved with origination of new guaranteed loans. The remaining 60 percent are involved with servicing delinquent guaranteed and portfolio loans, payment of lenders' claims due to foreclosure, and management and disposition of acquired property. For FY 1994, total VBA FTE would increase by 92 over FY 1993. The FY 1994 request for Loan Guaranty of 2,042 FTE represents a decrease of 2 percent in current program employment. This reduction reflects the Department's decision to reallocate staff from Loan Guaranty to Compensation and Pension. With these resources we will provide quality and timely service to veterans in FY 1994.

Mr. Chairman, this concludes my statement. I would be pleased to answer any questions which you or other members of the Subcommittee might have.

STATEMENT OF

CLIFTON E. DUPREE, ASSOCIATE LEGISLATIVE DIRECTOR

PARALYZED VETERANS OF AMERICA

BEFORE THE

SUBCOMMITTEE ON HOUSING, AND MEMORIAL AFFAIRS

OF THE

HOUSE COMMITTEE ON VETERANS' AFFAIRS

CONCERNING THE

VA GUARANTEED HOME LOAN PROGRAM

July 22, 1993

Mr. Chairman and Members of the Subcommittee, Paralyzed Veterans of America (PVA) thanks you for inviting us to testify today. I want to begin by conveying our gratitude for the time and effort you and the committee staff have devoted to this program. The existence of a viable benefit program to assist veterans in purchasing homes remains extremely important to the members of our organization.

Limited to accessible housing, individuals using wheelchairs are especially vulnerable to shifts in the national housing market. However, the Department of Veterans Affairs's (VA) Home Loan Guaranty Program has, without question, enabled many paralyzed veterans to fulfill their dreams of home ownership.

VA's offer of a fully guaranteed mortgage loan with no downpayment requirement has, for more than forty-seven years, allowed more than twelve million American veterans to purchase and maintain a home. VA regulations allow certain bankers to underwrite loans on an automatic basis, without VA prior approval. Eighty-five percent of all VA loans are underwritten automatically. VA has guaranteed more than 13.6 million loans since 1944, with 3.7 million loans presently outstanding.

Since the enactment of the "Veterans Home Loan Program Amendments of 1992," P.L. 102-547, the VA has guaranteed more than 2,000 Adjustable Rate Mortgages (ARMs) used by veterans to either purchase a home or refinance their present homes. The expansion of the VA Home Loan guaranty entitlement to certain members of the Reserve and National Guard has generated 900 new home loans, and the VA has issued more than 8,000 certificates of eligibility.

The Tribal Land Home Loan Program will provide VA direct loans to eligible Native American veterans to purchase, construct, or improve a home on Native American trust land. VA direct loans are limited to the cost of the home or $80,000, whichever is less. The tribal entity must have signed a Memorandum of Understanding (MOU) with the Secretary of Veterans Affairs which includes the conditions governing the tribal nations participation in the program.

However, no home loans have been made to Native American veterans living on trust lands. A MOU on the tribal land home loan program has been sent to all tribal nations for their review and approval. With the pending implementation of the program, it is more important than ever that resources become available such as those recommended in the FY 1994 **Independent Budget** for VA to have an additional one hundred thirteen FTEEs, including fifty for the VA loan servicing activities.

Mr. Chairman, the projected FY 1994 VA's Loan Guaranty budget is $83,647,000. While this is a modest increase over FY 1993 $81,063,000 appropriation, the loan servicing activities produce a large portion of that amount in program savings each year.

During FY 1992, VA's successful direct interventions on 5,029 properties resulted in an estimated $69 million in program savings. During the first two quarters of FY 1993, successful intervention on 2,500 properties has already resulted in an estimated program savings of $32.5 million. This equates to an annualized $48 million in direct program savings.

Perhaps equally important are the indirect savings to the government. When the VA regional office actively assists veterans through personal supplemental servicing they improve service to veteran borrowers in need of advice and assistance. The VA estimates that at least 500 foreclosures are avoided annually through personal supplemental servicing assistance which made direct intervention with the lender unnecessary.

During the last two years the home loan program's administration has improved significantly due to programs such as the "Federal Credit Reform Act of 1990." The principal objective of this act is to encourage and facilitate the extension of favorable credit terms by private lenders to veterans for the purchase, construction, or improvement of homes to be occupied by veterans and their families.

VA has established a monitoring unit to audit lenders. We cannot overvalue the importance of this oversight/audit activity because in approximately 87 percent of the cases lenders close on loans on an automatic basis, that is, without prior approval by VA. The inclusion of resale losses in net value used in the formula for determining whether VA will acquire foreclosed properties (the no-bid formula) continues to be a sound management practice; it deters lenders from making bad or marginal loans.

Mr. Chairman, this hearing, once again, shows your deep concern for the well-being of this important program and for the rights of the veterans who use it. This concludes my testimony. I will be pleased to answer any questions.

STATEMENT OF

DENNIS M. CULLINAN, DEPUTY DIRECTOR
NATIONAL LEGISLATIVE SERVICE
VETERANS OF FOREIGN WARS OF THE UNITED STATES

BEFORE THE

SUBCOMMITTEE ON HOUSING AND MEMORIAL AFFAIRS
COMMITTEE ON VETERANS' AFFAIRS
UNITED STATES HOUSE OF REPRESENTATIVES

WITH RESPECT TO

THE IMPLEMENTATION OF P.L. 102-547

WASHINGTON, DC   JULY 22, 1993

MR. CHAIRMAN AND MEMBERS OF THE SUBCOMMITTEE:

On behalf of the 2. 9 million members of the Veterans of Foreign Wars of the
United States and its Ladies Auxiliary, we wish to thank you for inviting us to take part in
today's hearing with respect to the VA Home Loan Program and the implementation of
P.L. 102-547. As you know, the VFW has been a staunch supporter of this highly
successful veterans' program through the years and we are both pleased and gratified to
play a role in today's discussion.

This veteran's program has guaranteed approximately 14 million home loans to
date and has proven to be tremendously beneficial for both veterans and the nation.
While providing this nation's veterans with the opportunity to achieve the America dream
of home ownership, it has also served as a mainstay of this nation's housing, construction
and banking industries. While serving America's veterans, the program has much
increased the tax base of communities throughout the nation while exercising a stabilizing
and revenue generating effect on both the banking and construction industries. It is
known that tax dollars invested in this program are multiplied many times and then turned
back into the American economy. This serves to greatly increase our national wealth by
enhancing the tax base and invigorating crucial industries.

As you are aware, P.L. 102-547 expanded VA loan guarantee entitlement to
certain members of the Reserve and National Guard; established an adjusted rate
mortgage program; permitted the Secretary to allow the veteran and the lender to
negotiate the interest rate on VA loans; and enabled the VA to make direct loans to
Native American veterans living on trusts lands. It is a matter of record that with the
exception of opening up a veterans home loan program to members of the Reserve and
National Guard who have not performed sufficient active duty service to be deemed
veterans under title 38, the VFW was supportive of this law to improve and enhance the
service the VA home loan program provides to America's veterans. Since Public Law

102-547 has been only recently enacted, we have accumulated little information from our membership regarding its effect on them. Even so, it is clear to us that this public law is highly beneficial and will certainly enhance the operation of the program. We would strongly recommend, however, that this public law be amended to allow for points to be rolled into the loan when a veteran refinances his home loan. It is clear from the language contained in the committee report on P.L. 102-547 that it was not the intention of the Congress to disallow rolling points into a refinanced loan, and that this was done inadvertently. We would now voice our strong support for remedial legislation.

As is stated in the letter of invitation, the Subcommittee also intends to focus today on loan servicing, property management, staffing levels, timeliness, and loan asset sales. In this regard, I cannot over emphasize the VFW's conviction that personal contact between a veteran borrower who has come upon financial hard times and VA is the most effective means of curing defaults. Successful intervention produces compassionate and cost-effective alternatives to foreclosure such as loan reinstatements, refunding, or voluntary conveyances (deed in lieu of foreclosure) for compromised claims. Additionally, VA can also sometimes arrange for the loan holder to grant a period of grace to a veteran who is suffering a temporary setback and who will soon be able to resume making loan payments. As indicated in the VSO's Independent Budget for VA, "rarely do the goals of deficit reduction, program integrity and efficiency and good service to veterans coincide so exactly as they do on improving loan servicing. " In FY 1992, for example, of the 153,389 defaults reported, 30,000 went to foreclosure. Thus, 70 percent of the bad loans were cured and veterans and their families remained in their own homes. This also resulted in large savings to the federal government during this period. In 1992 alone, VA saved $81 million. It is now estimated that savings resulting from loan servicing over the subsequent two years will result in savings of approximately $130 million.

The VA Home Loan Program represents a clear instance where an increase in FTEE will result in dramatic savings to the American tax payer rather than an increased burden. The VFW recommends the addition of 50 employees to the program. This would greatly benefit VA loan servicing activities. The resultant savings due to increased intervention activity and a higher cure rate will more than offset their salaries. Further, even more veterans, who for one reason or another are temporarily delinquent in making their loan payments, will be spared the trauma and financial hardship of a foreclosure and be enabled to keep themselves and their families in their own homes.

Mr. Chairman, once again, I wish to thank you on behalf of the entire membership of the Veterans of Foreign Wars for inviting us to participate in today's important hearing.

The VFW remains committed to the continuing and enhanced operation of the VA Home Loan Program as it serves America's veterans. A germane resolution is appended to this statement for your review. This concludes my statement, and I would be happy to respond to any questions you may have.

Resolution No. 623

VA HOME LOAN GUARANTY PROGRAM

WHEREAS, VA Home Loan Guaranty Program is one of the most popular and beneficial programs available to veterans; and

WHEREAS, the wide use of this program is evidenced by the fact that over 13 million loans have been guaranteed to date in an amount exceeding $300 billion; and

WHEREAS, loan origination fees have been enacted and subsequently increased in an effort to remedy the ailing revolving fund; and

WHEREAS, constructive changes have been implemented or proposed in the VA Home Loan Guaranty Program, such as granting the Secretary the authority to (a) independently set loan interest rates; (b) improve the formula for establishing the loan guaranty percentage/maximum amount; (c) provide mortgage payment assistance to avoid foreclosure; (d) amend VA foreclosure policy to enhance VA Loan Guaranty Revolving Fund, hence strengthening the program; and (e) provide indemnification against debt to VA in the event of foreclosure; now, therefore

BE IT RESOLVED, by the 93rd National Convention of the Veterans of Foreign Wars of the United States, that legislation be introduced that will serve to maintain VA Home Loan Guaranty Program as the most viable and desirable means of home financing for veterans; and

BE IT FURTHER RESOLVED, that the Veterans of Foreign Wars vigorously opposes any effort to further increase the current loan origination fee or eliminate VA established loan interest maximum.

Adopted by the 93rd National Convention of the Veterans of Foreign Wars of the United States, held in Indianapolis, Indiana, August 14-21, 1992.

Resolution No. 623

STATEMENT OF
RICHARD F. SCHULTZ
ASSISTANT NATIONAL LEGISLATIVE DIRECTOR
OF THE
DISABLED AMERICAN VETERANS
BEFORE THE
SUBCOMMITTEE ON HOUSING AND MEMORIAL AFFAIRS
OF THE
COMMITTEE ON VETERANS AFFAIRS
U.S. HOUSE OF REPRESENTATIVES
JULY 22, 1993

MR. CHAIRMAN AND MEMBERS OF THE SUBCOMMITTEE:

On behalf of the more than 1.3 million members of the
Disabled American Veterans (DAV) and its Women's Auxiliary, I
wish to thank you for the opportunity to present our views
relative to the implementation of Public Law 102-547, the
"Veterans' Home Loan Program Improvements Act of 1992." We also
appreciate the Subcommittee focusing its attention on loan
servicing, property management, staffing levels, timeliness and
loan asset sales and are pleased to present our views on these
important issues.

Mr. Chairman, at the outset, we wish to commend you and the
members of the Subcommittee for the timely exercise of your
oversight responsibilities. In addition, we acknowledge and
applaud the members of the Subcommittee for your outstanding
advocacy on behalf of America's veterans. Clearly, had it not
been for the advocacy of this Subcommittee, loan guaranteed
benefits available to America's veteran population would have
been significantly eroded.

Public Law 102-547, "Veterans' Home Loan Program Improvements Act of 1992."

Mr. Chairman, with your permission, I will now address
those provisions of Public Law 102-547 identified in your letter
of invitation dated June 25, 1993.

Major provisions of the measure include:

* Expanding entitlement, during the period from
October 1, 1992, to September 30, 1992, to the VA Home
Loan Guaranty Program to members of the National Guard
and Reserves who have received an honorable discharge
or have served at least six years. Additionally,
Guard and Reserve members are required to pay an
indemnity fee that is .75 percent above those paid by
veterans who derive their loan guarantee eligibility
as a result of active military service.

Mr. Chairman, we have been advised that during the period
of November 1992 through April 1993, there were 855 loans
guaranteed by VA for members of the National Guard and
Reserves. In addition, 8,300 certificates of eligibility have
been issued by VA to this new category of VA loan guarantee
eligibles. While DAV has no National Convention mandate
pertaining to National Guard and Reservist loan guarantee
eligibility, we certainly understand the intent of Congress to
recognize the contribution made by members of the Guard and
Reserves. We also understand that the use of VA's Loan Guaranty
entitlement is increasing each month as more and more Guard and
Reservists become aware of this new entitlement. Our only
concern is that VA Loan Guaranty have enough employees to handle
the increase in workload associated with this new Loan Guaranty
entitlement.

* Establishment of a three-year Pilot Program during
Fiscal Years 1993, 1994, and 1995 on Adjustable Rate
Mortgages (ARMs) at VA Regional Offices, and require

the Secretary to submit annual reports on this
program. Additionally, the annual interest rate
adjustments will be limited to no more than one
percentage point higher or lower than the rate charged
at the time of the adjustment, and the maximum
interest rate at any time during the term of the loan
would be limited to no more than five percentage
points above the initial rate.

VA has advised us that there have been more than 2,400 VA
home loan guarantees using an adjustable rate mortgage. DAV has
received no reports (neither positive or negative) from our
members regarding adjustable rate mortgages.

* Establish a three-year Pilot Program to permit, at the
discretion of the Secretary, veteran/lender negotiated
VA guaranteed loan interest rates.

Mr. Chairman, we also have received no complaints regarding
veteran/lender negotiated interest rates.

* A requirement that the VA, from October 1, 1992, until
December 31, 1994, establish and implement a Pilot
Program whereby the VA may make direct housing loans
to native American veterans and permit such veterans
to purchase, construct, or improve dwellings on trust
land.

Mr. Chairman, we understand that VA intends to issue
interim final regulations on this program soon and final
regulations within two months. Additionally, a memorandum of
understanding with two tribal organizations is ready for
signature and VA expects to start processing applications for
direct loans to native American veterans within six weeks.

We believe that the Native American Veteran Home Loan Pilot
Program has the potential to provide a meaningful benefit to an
underserved population of American veterans. We applaud the
Subcommittee's efforts in this regard and look forward to
implementation of this program.

*   *   *

Mr. Chairman, in the area of loan servicing, VA has made
great strides over the past several years. Currently, nearly 38
percent (750) of VA's Loan Guaranty field staff is dedicated to
loan servicing.

Effective loan servicing just makes good sense! In human
terms, proper loan servicing can prevent a veteran and his or her
family from becoming another homeless statistic. In economic
terms, it saves tax payers' money.

During Fiscal Year 1992, VA successfully intervened in
5,029 loan defaults, saving more than $69,000,000. The
statistics for the first half of Fiscal Year 1993 show a repeat
of last year.

Mr. Chairman, in June of 1992, VA had 14,225 properties on
hand; by June of this year, that number had dropped to 12,322.
In an effort to reduce VA's housing inventory, VA is engaged in
a number of activities which include: paid advertising,
outreach to realtors, and seminars for the real estate
community. In addition, VA has made use of computer technology,
such as the bulletin board, in certain high-volume areas of the
country in an effort to apprise would-be buyers of the
availability of VA properties.

Mr. Chairman, we commend VA for its efforts in the property
management area and would hope that they continue to expand
their efforts to reduce the large number of properties in their
inventory.

We understand that there has been a slight increase in Loan Guaranty processing time. This is due, in part, to increased loan activity. During the first eight months of Fiscal Year 1993, VA closed 228,433 loans compared to 157,459 during the same period last year. This large increase in loan activity is primarily due to low interest rates and the corresponding increase in refinanced loans.

The Loan Appraisal Process (LAP) Program which began in Fiscal Year 1992, is starting to reap dividends. For the period of April 1, 1992, through March 31, 1993, there were 7,374 determinations of reasonable value processed using LAP. The LAP system, which allows lenders to expedite the scheduling of appraisals, together with the automated value determinations in which appraisals are sent directly to lenders rather than going through VA, improves timeliness and frees up VA employees to do other loan guarantee activities.

With respect to VA's efforts regarding loan asset sales, we wish to note that as a result of Public Law 102-291, VA is now authorized to directly guarantee the principal and interest on mortgage securities issued as a result of VA vendee loan sales. This new authority has enhanced the market value of VA loan asset sales. In February 1992, VA realized increased income for loan asset sales of $12.5 million. Thus far in Fiscal Year 1993, VA has realized a nearly $20 million increase in revenue due to the enhancements made by Public Law 102-291. We are pleased to also note that Public Law 102-547 extended the enhanced loan asset sale authorities through 1995.

Finally, Mr. Chairman, we wish to draw your attention to the Independent Budget (IB) for Fiscal Year 1994. The IB has recommended an increase of 50 employees in the loan servicing area. As previously pointed out, effective loan servicing reaps dividends in both human and economic terms. Additionally, the IB requests an overall loan guarantee employment level of 2,180 -- 105 over the current level.

In closing, Mr. Chairman, I wish to again thank you and the members of the Subcommittee for requesting our views on these important issues. I would be happy to answer any questions you or members of the Subcommittee may have.

STATEMENT OF
MICHAEL P. CLINE (RET)
MASTER SERGEANT

EXECUTIVE DIRECTOR

BEFORE THE
HOUSE VETERANS' AFFAIRS SUBCOMMITTEE

ON

HOUSING AND MEMORIAL AFFAIRS

22 JULY 1993

We are pleased to have the opportunity to submit testimony before the Veteran's Affairs Subcommittee on Housing and Memorial Affairs. We proudly express the views of the 63,000 members of the Enlisted Association of the National Guard of the United States (EANGUS).

EANGUS represents the Enlisted members of the Army and Air National Guard and their views on important issues which affect the National Guard. We would like to report EANGUS's position on the progress of Public Law 102-547.

We have received several calls from National Guard members indicating that the implementation of the Law is positive and they are pleased. However, the majority of our members who have contacted us are wondering if the law has been implemented. The information going out to both the Veteran's Administration office in the field and Realtors on the program was slow to be released, therefore, many EANGUS members are unaware of the status of the Law. We are unable to give an accurate account of National Guard member's positions on the progress of the Law at this time due to the delayed release of information.

The current state of the economy and the housing market are tenuous at best. EANGUS does not claim to be an expert in financial management. However, adjustable rate mortgages appear to be an enhancing factor in the home loan program.

The loan program is intended for military personnel to make an investment in a home and also to assist them in adjusting to civilian life. The largest portion of the military is enlisted personnel and many have limited financial resources. Retirees, often dealing with a fixed income, are another primary user the program.

Adjustable Rate Mortgages are good for the younger buyer by giving them the opportunity to enter the housing market at a level beyond their current means but within their anticipated means. This not only allows individuals to purchase homes earlier but also provides them with the most affordable rates. Any program that will enhance National Guard members' ability to realize the American dream of owning a home and reduce the costs of doing so will be endorsed by EANGUS.

National Guard and Reserve forces are progressively playing a greater role in our country's defense--the Persian Gulf being a classic example. With the changing world picture and a lessening in the number of active duty members in the regular armed forces, Reservists and National Guard members will play a greater role in our nation's defense.

Public Law 102-547 also established and implemented a pilot program under which direct housing loans could be made to Native Americans. Native Americans continue to make important military contributions.
Native Americans, like National Guard members and Reservists, have served proudly and deserve the opportunity to cut out the financial middleman. After all, this country is their native land.

It is well known that staff shortages in the VA Department's offices throughout the country negatively affect the operation of the Va Home Loan Guaranty Program. The Veteran's Administration must be sufficiently staffed to handle a plan the size of the VA Home Loan Bill. Many complications can arise with a program of this size that need to be dealt with promptly in order for things to run efficiently. Program losses and processing delays could often be avoided if appropriate staff levels were provided. It is EANGUS's belief that the VA should maintain a staff that can manage the VA home loan program along with all other VA programs.

In summary, EANGUS supports recognition of the value of National Guard service and equity in determining eligibility for benefits. The National Guard and Reserve make a major contribution to the defense of this nation, as

43

demonstrated by Operation Desert Shield/Desert Storm. National Guard service represents a cost effective way to maximize defense capability. Authorizing National Guard members, Reserves, and Native American veterans participation in the Veterans' home loan program makes a tangible contribution toward strengthening America. In addition, it helps a valued benefit program.

STATEMENT OF

VIETNAM VETERANS OF AMERICA

Presented By

Paul S. Egan
Executive Director

Before The

House Veterans' Affairs Subcommittee On Housing and Memorial Affairs

On

VA Loan Guaranty Program

July 22, 1993

TABLE OF CONTENTS

Introduction

Mr. Chairman and members of the Subcommittee, Vietnam Veterans of America (VVA), appreciates the opportunity to present its views on various aspects of the VA Loan Guaranty Program. Many veterans have depended on this program to achieve home ownership. And many veterans falsely believe the VA will act on their behalf if economic difficulties arise and the veteran borrower defaults on the loan.

This program needs the stringent oversight of this Subcommittee, Mr. Chairman, both to ensure that veterans' best interests are served in the program and to ensure that the VA implements its duties in a manner that benefits veterans without resulting in excessive expenditure of taxpayer funds. Your interest specifically in our evaluation of VA's implementation of Public Law 102-547, is very relevant to some of the concerns we have raised in the past. And we are pleased to have the opportunity to discuss with this Subcommittee the issues of loan servicing, staffing levels and timeliness, as well as property management and loan asset sales.

Is the New Law Working?

Although it is still too soon after enactment of the new law for emergence of meaningful data useful for evaluating the success or failure of Public Law 102-547,

VVA would like to present a few thoughts on what questions such an evaluat: should answer. The intent of last year's legislation, as we understand it, was to g veterans more bargaining power for arranging a mortgage and purchasing a hoi Several of the provisions included in this law, such as adjustable rate mortga (ARMs), veteran-borrower payment of points and the ability to negotiate with lend for interest rates, were already available to the general population of home bu· and patrons of other government loan guaranty programs. Presumably, tl measures were intended to help more veterans achieve home ownership. There three specific questions that must be asked·in evaluating the effectiveness of t measures once the data are in.

First, since the enactment of this law, has the VA been able either to ex the percentage of its marketshare among mortgage lenders or expand the numl eligible veterans actually using their VA home loan guaranty entitlement tha: the case before the new law was enacted? The loan provisions mentioned abo well as expanded entitlement to certain members of the Reserves and Na Guard, the authority for VA to make direct loans to Native American ve· residing on trust lands, and the reduced refinancing fees and availability of I Efficient Mortgages, were designed to make VA guaranteed loans more appeali to expand the eligibility for such loans. VA should be able to compile stati: evaluate whether or not this has in fact happened. If, in fact, this has not ha at least one of the presumably intended purposes of the new law has failed.

Secondly and more importantly, did this law in effect allow veterans to borrow more than they can reasonably afford? VVA has always contended that the VA does veterans a disservice if the loan guaranty terms allow a veteran borrower to assume a mortgage beyond his or her means. This is often the cause of defaults, although little on this point is conceded by bankers, realtors or others with a proprietary stake in the VA home loan program. If the provisions of P.L. 102-547 give veterans more bargaining power such that they borrow too much money, it will become evident in a few years that the default rate increased for loans authorized under this law. Similarly, have veterans been able to successfully negotiate favorable interest rates applied to their mortgages with lenders? How do rates subsequent to the new law compare with rates prior to the law?

And finally this Subcommittee should ask, has this law improved the receptiveness of lending institutions willing to process VA guaranteed loans? Veterans presumably were having difficulty finding a mortgage company willing to handle or process VA guaranteed loans. P.L. 102-547 was supposed to deregulate VA guaranteed loan requirements, to meet current industry standards. If in fact this has happened, it would seem that lenders should be more willing to work with the VA. Are they, and if so, what is and where is the evidence?

Loan Servicing, Staffing and Timeliness

Anyone involved in veterans advocacy can cite many horror stories of woefully inadequate VA loan servicing at the Regional Office level. This, in addition to improperly qualifying veterans prior to lending to them, is evidenced in the dismal default and foreclosure statistics of VA guaranteed mortgages. Lately VA has seen fit to defend its loan servicing performance by bandying around statistics indicating between 72 and 74 percent of all defaults were corrected in 1992. Naturally we are expected to assume that this is due directly to the efforts of VA loan servicing. VA is silent, however, on the fact that only about 7 percent of the cured defaults resulted from any VA loan service assistance whatsoever. The remainder are cases in which the veteran borrower brought the loan current himself or herself by simply paying the arrears to the lender.

In FY 1992, VA was notified by lending institutions of approximately 150,000 defaults. Approximately 30,000 of these defaults ended in foreclosures. This leaves 120,000 defaults which were reinstated. The VA claims on this basis a ratio of four to one reinstatements to foreclosures, or a 72 to 74 percent success rate.

If only this were true, we would have nothing but glowing praise for the hard work of VA's loan servicing operations. Sadly, however, the truth behind VA's efforts to mislead shows a dramatically different picture of loan servicing efforts by VA. The

50

fact is that VA's loan servicing efforts accounted, at best, for only 7 percent of all reinstatements in FY 1992. What VA fails to tell you is that of the 120,000 reinstatements, it had a hand in only 8,599 (7 %). These included 920 refundings, 1,959 deeds in lieu of foreclosure, 691 compromise claims, and approximately 5,029 successful interventions of one kind or another (920 + 1,959 + 691 + 5,029 = 8,599). Therefore, VA can only take honest credit for 8,599 reinstatements or 7 percent. By attempting to claim significant credit for the remaining 111,400, or 93 percent, the VA has engaged in deceitfulness of staggering magnitude.

In general, we are all aware of the severe understaffing of VA Regional Offices which causes backlogs and delays for the processing of veteran claims in everything from compensation and pensions to vocational rehabilitation and education program eligibility. Staffing problems with the loan guaranty service are no different. Certainly we can all agree that many VA Regional Offices and their veteran clients could benefit from improved timeliness and hopefully responsiveness that would result from increased staffing and training at Regional Offices. Barring unlimited funding though, there are organizational structure improvements for the Loan Guaranty Service that we propose and call to your attention.

It seems logical, and we believe lending institutions would agree, that the VA Loan Guaranty Service should establish one central location for filing and data entry coding of default notifications and lender letters of intention to foreclose. This would free Regional Office staff for other loan servicing responsibilities, and would undoubtedly be more convenient for lending institutions. Other functions could perhaps be similarly structured, utilizing a few staff in a central location--in effect establishing economies of scale to simplify processing. For instance, we understand that there is a backlog in the issuance of guaranty certificates; sales have been closed and the veteran already resides in the home long before the guaranty certificate is issued. By centralizing the paper shuffling functions, VA home loan officials could become free to provide loan servicing functions.

Refunding Less Costly than Foreclosure

As you know, Mr. Chairman, VVA has worked closely with Representatives Lane Evans and Joe Kennedy to develop legislation which would address this issue in a meaningful way by statutorily obligating VA to carry out a set of procedures for consideration of refunding (refinancing) applications of veterans in default. While there are other methods VA may utilize to prevent foreclosure, namely deeds in lieu of foreclosure, compromise claims and direct intervention with the lender, refunding should be, but is not, an important additional tool in VA's loan servicing efforts.

We are pleased to endorse H.R. 2331, legislation sponsored by Representatives Lane Evans and Joe Kennedy, which has been tailored to address the dual problems which veterans encounter in the current system when through no fault of their own they default on their VA-guaranteed mortgage and the VA fails to perform the safeguarding steps necessary to assist the veteran in keeping his or her home.

Countless cases come to our attention of veterans who are needlessly thrown out of their homes when they are laid off from work or become disabled, and are either temporarily unable to make mortgage payments or are short of sufficient funds due to replacement of job income at a lower wage, as is often the case with laid off industrial workers.

In addition, foreclosure is very costly for the federal government; $2.2 billion in appropriations was required to cover the cost of acquiring nearly 208,813 deeds following foreclosure between fiscal years 1984 and 1989. In most instances, as you may not know, the VA acquires the deed from the lender after foreclosure, and takes responsibility and risk of selling the property. Exercising its option to acquire the loan instead of the deed after foreclosure and refinancing that loan would certainly be no more costly to the VA, as the full property value would be recovered when the loan term is completed. The VA would gain an interest bearing asset, rather than a property management liability.

53

Property Management and Loan Sales

Nearly all foreclosed mortgages become part of the VA property management portfolio. Once the deed rather than the income generating loan becomes a possession of the VA, a new round of needless mismanagement costs taxpayers billions of additional dollars. When VA subsequently resells the property, the agency either receives cash (a cash sale) or receives a promise from a buyer to pay a certain amount to the Government (a term sale). Term sales become portfolio loans.

Buyer debts (term sales) are secured by VA in an installment contract, mortgage or a deed of trust. Installment contracts, on one hand, are easy to terminate if the buyer defaults on the loan. Termination of a mortgage or deed of trust, on the other hand, usually requires a foreclosure, involving a several step process initiated by the Regional Office. The Loan Guaranty Division must request the assistance of VA's District Counsel who, in turn, requests the assistance of either the U.S. Attorney or a fee attorney to foreclose a defaulted mortgage or deed of trust. Many VA portfolio loans in foreclosure remain non-productive Government assets because either the Regional Office Loan Guaranty Divisions and/or because District Counsel Offices, U.S. Attorney Offices or fee attorneys fail to pursue foreclosure in a timely manner.

The VA quarterly report entitled Portfolio Loan System Loans in Foreclosure

8

(COIN PLS 29-01), for the period ending April 30, 1993, cites examples of this mismanagement: in your home state of Illinois, Mr. Chairman, there are 31 portfolio loans 12 or more months delinquent, ranging all the way up to one loan 54 months delinquent for a loss to the government of $22,458.60; in Mr. Burton's state of Indiana, there are 38 loans 24 or more months delinquent, the longest at 105 months, and the highest value loss of $36,165.35; statistics are similarly abominable for the remaining states. We would be happy to share this report with this Subcommittee. These are loans that the VA wants to foreclose, as they are listed in this report, but inaction has allowed the properties be inhabited essentially rent free. This report says nothing of the thousands of delinquent loans that VA has not yet referred to its own District Counsel for foreclosure. Who knows what the net tax-dollar loss is for loans in this category?

Mr. Chairman, all of this goes to prove once again that the VA is not only unwilling to assist veterans as it is mandated to do, but it also lacks the sense to take steps necessary to save scarce taxpayer resources. With regard to VA's management of its portfolio loans, the process it uses deserves your careful attention. As you have stated in expressing your reservations about creating an adjudications process for veterans applying for VA refinancing under the terms of the Evans/Kennedy bill, the more appropriate target of your criticism is the process used by VA in disposing of delinquent portfolio loans.

To rectify this problem of gross mismanagement, as well as to assuage your concerns about adjudications for loan refinancing, we once again draw your attention to the carefully tailored provisions of H.R. 2331. Under provisions of this bill, these portfolio loans can be swiftly terminated, the properties resold by VA, and the revolving funds replenished either by keeping current active loans in VA's portfolio, or by selling current active loans in VA's loan sales. In order to prevent future taxpayer loss due to mismanagement, the VA should sell more of its properties using installment contract arrangements as currently authorized by law, or obtain unrecorded quit claim deeds from borrowers at the time of sale or refunding as would be authorized under the terms of H.R. 2331.

Mr. Chairman, this concludes our testimony.

TESTIMONY OF
THE NATIONAL ASSOCIATION OF REALTORS®
BEFORE THE
U.S. HOUSE OF REPRESENTATIVES
COMMITTEE ON VETERANS AFFAIRS
SUBCOMMITTEE ON
HOUSING AND MEMORIAL AFFAIRS
on the
VA HOME LOAN GUARANTY PROGRAM

JULY 22, 1993

INTRODUCTION

Mr. Chairman, Members of the Subcommittee, the NATIONAL ASSOCIATION OF REALTORS® appreciates the opportunity to submit written testimony regarding various aspects of Public Law 102-547, the Veterans Home Loan Program Amendments of 1992. The NATIONAL ASSOCIATION OF REALTORS® represents a wide variety of housing industry professionals committed to the development and preservation of the nation's housing stock and making it available to the widest range of potential homebuyers.

The NATIONAL ASSOCIATION OF REALTORS® has been a strong supporter of, and major participant in, the VA Home Loan Guaranty Program since its inception. More recently, the NATIONAL ASSOCIATION OF REALTORS® worked diligently for the passage of P.L.102-547 to improve the availability and affordability of veterans' housing, strongly supporting its provisions revitalizing the program and making it competitive with other mortgage products. The Association continues to believe in the viability of the program, and we commend the Subcommittee for providing continued improvements to ensure that the program fulfills its objective of helping veterans buy and remain in their homes.

The NATIONAL ASSOCIATION OF REALTORS® is particularly grateful for the Subcommittee's leadership this session in achieving full Committee approval of legislation (H.R.949) increasing the amount in VA home loan guaranty. The NATIONAL ASSOCIATION OF REALTORS® testified before the Subcommittee in strong support of the initiative increasing the amount a veteran is eligible to borrow -- from $184,000 to $203,000 -- which provides welcome relief to qualified veteran buyers in high-priced areas who previously had difficulty obtaining VA loans.

Mr. Chairman, the NATIONAL ASSOCIATION OF REALTORS® applauds the continuing commitment of the Subcommittee to promote affordable housing opportunities for our nation's veterans. Through its Residential Finance Subcommittee of the Real Estate Finance Committee, the NATIONAL ASSOCIATION OF REALTORS® monitors all aspects of government mortgage programs including the DVA Home Loan Guaranty Program. At its most recent meeting, the 1993 MidYear Conference in April, the Residential Finance Subcommittee expressed no misgivings with any aspect of the home loan program.

Although it is too soon after enactment of P.L.102-547 for the emergence of meaningful evaluation data, we believe the changes enacted under the new law coupled with eventual passage of H.R.949 will reinvigorate VA's share of the housing market in all segments of the country. The NATIONAL ASSOCIATION OF REALTORS® is actively promoting the new changes throughout the veteran community and real estate industry, and we welcome the opportunity to share our early observations on the following key provisions.

1.   Reservists' Eligibility for DVA Home Loan Guaranty Program

P.L.102-547 extended loan guaranty benefits, for the first time, to reservists under certain conditions. Previously, VA guaranteed home loans were limited to active duty veterans and individuals on active duty who satisfied the requirements for eligibility contained in Title 38, Chapter 37, United States Code. Under the new law, individuals who have completed six years of service in the nation's reserve forces are eligible. A funding fee of 2 percent is required, and can be reduced to 1.5 percent with a 5 percent downpayment or 1.25 percent with a 10 percent downpayment.

The NATIONAL ASSOCIATION OF REALTORS® wholeheartedly welcomed the extension of loan guaranty benefits to reservists in recognition of their service and dedication to our Nation. We anticipate a substantial increase in the volume of VA loan originations because of this important change. We believe reservists' eligibility will renew the life of the home loan guaranty program and help bolster the financial condition of the DVA Guaranty and Indemnity Fund.

Equally important, the NATIONAL ASSOCIATION OF REALTORS® foresees an increase in loan volume translating into a corresponding increase of VA mortgage pools securitized by the Government National Mortgage Association (Ginnie Mae) that will help boost its overall loan production. Historically VA mortgages have only accounted for a small portion of the collateral going into Ginnie Mae mortgage-backed securities. However, tightened underwriting associated with FHA's mortgage program coupled with the new changes mandated by P.L.102-547 are resulting in VA loans comprising a significant share of new Ginnie Mae pools.

2.   DVA Negotiated Interest Rate

The NATIONAL ASSOCIATION OF REALTORS® is particularly pleased with the decision of Congress to change, albeit temporary, from an administered to a negotiated interest rate in which the veteran is now on a level playing field with other home purchasers. The NATIONAL ASSOCIATION OF REALTORS® recognizes that the change to a negotiated interest rate is a major turning point in the history of VA financing and constitutes a major revision to a long-standing basic provision of the home loan program. However, we believe the new change will permit more veterans than ever to realize the dream of homeownership because the law now allows VA borrowers to negotiate with lenders for the most favorable rate and terms available.

The NATIONAL ASSOCIATION OF REALTORS® believes the new change will make VA financing much more attractive to sellers now that the points are negotiable and may be paid by the borrower, and we strongly encourage its adoption as a permanent feature of the VA home loan program. Further, the NATIONAL ASSOCIATION OF REALTORS® encourages Congress to restore the veteran's ability to finance discount points, a technical omission that has been amended and is currently pending under H.R.949 which we strongly support.

The NATIONAL ASSOCIATION OF REALTORS® has adamantly maintained that the administered rate was disadvantageous to the potential veteran home buyer because it limited the veteran's choices of housing availability and inadvertently restricted the veteran from utilizing his or her entitlement. The NATIONAL ASSOCIATION OF REALTORS® recognized and appreciated the rationale of the administered rate -- to protect veteran borrowers from being overcharged and to ensure that veterans were not paying a rate in excess of the VA maximum. However, the administered rate often lagged the market, forcing lenders to charge a greater number of discount points to improve their yields and make the VA loans more attractive to investors.

Since VA borrowers were prohibited by law as to the maximum number of discount points they could pay, homeowners selling their homes to veteran buyers were often forced to pay the discount points. In many instances, sellers were wary of would-be veteran borrowers and chose not to offer VA financing.

3.   Demonstration Adjustable Rate Mortgage (ARM) Program

P.L.102-547 provides for the establishment of an adjustable rate mortgage product within the DVA. The VA ARM program provides for a maximum annual interest rate increase of 1 percent and a 5 percent life of the loan limit on rate increases. To reduce the potential risk of rising rates, the DVA is requiring that applications for ARM loans be underwritten at 1 percentage point above the initial interest rate. This authority is for a 3-year period ending December 31, 1995.

The NATIONAL ASSOCIATION OF REALTORS® has long advocated and supported an ARM product for our nation's veterans because it increases the veteran's opportunities for home ownership and facilitates the different borrowing needs of veteran borrowers. Additionally, a VA ARM program complements the FHA ARM which received permanent authority from Congress several years ago to insure ARMs. The NATIONAL ASSOCIATION OF REALTORS® is pleased to know the DVA has modeled its product after the FHA ARM, and we strongly encourage Congress to extend permanent authority in behalf of the VA ARM as well.

Clearly, FHA ARMs are the most popular adjustable rate products on the market today because of their advantageous consumer features. Whereas most conventional ARMs may limit annual interest rate increases to two percentage points and increases over the life of the loan to six points, FHA ARMs cap annual and life-of-the-loan interest rate adjustments to just one and five percentage points, respectively. Notwithstanding the higher one percentage point VA ARM rate to offset any unexpected increase in mortgage rates, introduction of the VA ARM product patterned after FHA's ARM could not occur at a more advantageous moment for the veteran because many lenders are currently offering adjustables at extremely low rates.

CONCLUSION

The NATIONAL ASSOCIATION OF REALTORS® appreciates this opportunity to submit written testimony on oversight of Public Law 102-547, the Veterans Home Loan Program Amendments of 1992. We believe the modifications enacted by Congress are resulting in an increase in VA loan origination volume and are helping to revitalize the program and reinvigorate VA's share of the housing market to the benefit of our veterans.

The NATIONAL ASSOCIATION OF REALTORS® welcomes the opportunity to work with Congress to enhance the VA Home Loan Guaranty Program and we applaud this Subcommittee for its efforts promoting homeownership for our nation's veterans.

○